If at First...

The answer to the riddle below is easy, if you know your measurements. Each "if" statement will give you a letter and tell you where to put it. Fill in all the letters, and you will have your answer—no ifs, ands, or buts!

a. If a cup is larger than a pint, the third letter is a **U**. If not, it is an **O**.

b. If there are 100 centimeters in a meter, the first and tenth letters are **A**. If not, they are **I**.

c. If a liter is smaller than a gallon, the last letter is an **R**. If not, it is a **T**.

d. If there are three teaspoons in a tablespoon, the sixth letter is an **L**. If not, it is a **D**.

e. If there are 5,000 pounds in a ton, the seventh, ninth, and twelfth letters are **C**. If not, they are **E**.

f. If there are 1,000 grams in a kilogram, the fourth letter is a **U**. If not, it is a **V**.

g. If there are seven feet in two yards, the eighth letter is an **A**. If not, it is an **H**.

h. If a mile is longer than a kilometer, the fifth letter is a **B**. If not, it is a **T**.

i. If 1,000 millimeters equals 1 centimeter, the second and eleventh letters are **B**. If not, they are **D**.

What do you get when you cross a monster and a baseball game?

___ ___ ___ ___ ___ ___ ___ ___ ___ ___ ___ ___ ___
1   2   3   4   5   6   7   8   9   10   11   12   13

What's Your Dog IQ?

Are you a friend of Fido? A bestie to Barkly? Circle your answers and see how many you can fetch in this canine quiz.

1. What is a schnoodle?
a. A mix between a Schnauzer and a poodle
b. A mix between a poodle and a sheepdog
c. A long buttery noodle

2. At birth, Dalmatians are:
a. Completely white
b. Completely black
c. Red-and-green striped

3. The greyhound is the fastest type of dog on the planet. How fast can they run?
a. 30 miles per hour
b. 45 miles per hour
c. Faster than the speed of light

4. Dogs can see best in what type of light?
a. Bright light
b. Low light
c. Strobe lights

5. The Newfoundland has this unique characteristic:
a. Webbed feet
b. No tail
c. Ability to hula hoop

6. Normal adult dogs have how many teeth?
a. 32
b. 42
c. 144

7. Dogs only sweat from one place. What is it?
a. Pads of their feet
b. Nose
c. Collar

Illustrated by Dave Klug

Doggie Dilemma

Diego is getting a new dog! You can help him choose a breed. Use the clues below to cross off breeds on Diego's list. Can you figure out which kind of dog Diego will pick?

CLUES

1. The breed has a name with exactly 3 vowels.

2. The name of the breed has 2 vowels side by side.

3. There is at least one letter *a* in the name of the breed.

4. There is an even number of letters in the breed's name.

Diego's List

Akita	Doberman
Basset hound	Great Dane
Beagle	Husky
Bloodhound	Maltese
Boxer	Poodle
Bulldog	Pug
Chihuahua	Retriever
Chow chow	Sheepdog
Collie	Spaniel
Dalmatian	Terrier

Unidentified UFOs!

UFO usually stands for Unidentified Flying Object. But each of these clues describes a different UFO! Can you identify all the matches? We did the first one for you.

1. Large, sad, flightless bird in Paris

2. Lint-covered breakfast food

3. Wise winged girls in the city

4. Unattractive hopping robber

5. Root vegetable from Tallahassee

6. Hilarious policeman

7. Icy and pristine Atlantic

a. Ugly Frog Outlaw

b. Undisturbed Frozen Ocean

c. Upper Florida Onion

d. Unhappy French Ostrich

e. Unbelievably Funny Officer

f. Urban Female Owls

g. Untouched Fuzzy Oatmeal

Answers: 1. d, 2. g, 3. f, 4. a, 5. c, 6. e, 7. b

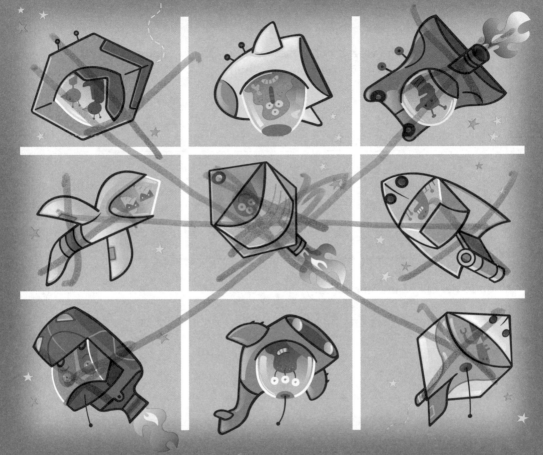

Tic Tac Row

Each of these spaceships has something in common with the other two spaceships in the same row. For example, in the first row across all three spaceships have antennae on top. Look at the other rows across, down, and diagonally. Can you tell what's alike in each row?

Sy Wht?!?

Just for fun, we left the vowels out of these words. Can you figure out each word? Each group has something in common, but what?

1.

BRD _____

PLN _____

HLCPTR _____

BTTRFLY _____

MSQT _____

DRGNFLY _____

What do they have in common?

_____

2.

PNNY _____

BSBLL _____

FLL MN _____

DGHNT _____

BLBRRY _____

SMLY FC _____

What do they have in common?

_____

Illustrated by Kelly Kennedy

Answers: 1. bird, plane, helicopter, butterfly, mosquito, dragonfly; They can all fly. 2. penny, baseball, full moon, doughnut, blueberry, smiley face; They are all round.

Say What?

Texting Tessie loves to be brief. To her, there are 60 S in a M. That's 60 seconds in a minute to the rest of us. Can you figure out some more of Tessie's shortcuts?

1. 60 S in a M ___**60 seconds in a minute**___

2. 7 D in a W _____

3. 12 I in a F _____

4. 12 M in a Y _____

5. 4 Q in a G _____

6. 2 C in a P _____

7. 60 M in an H _____

8. 3 F in a Y _____

9. 24 H in a D _____

10. 26 L in the A _____

11. 52 W in a Y _____

12. 365 D in a Y _____

13. 100 Y in a C _____

14. 52 C in a D _____

15. 50 S on the U.S. F _____

Illustrated by Wendy Wax

Rain Forest Funnies

How do you catch a monkey?
>   *Climb a tree and act like a banana.*

What do you say to a tree frog who needs a ride?
>   *"Hop in!"*

Which side of a parrot has the prettiest feathers?
>   *The outside.*

What do tigers sing in December?
>   *"Jungle Bells, Jungle Bells!"*

How do monkeys get down the stairs?
>   *They slide down the bananaster!*

What snakes are found on cars?
>   *Windshield vipers.*

What do you get if you cross a parrot and a shark?
>   *A bird that talks your ear off.*

What is the silliest name you could give a tiger?
>   *Spot.*

Rain Forest Q's

Illustrated by Mike Moran
Puzzles by Carly Schuna

Rain Forest Quiz
Match each question to the right answer.

1. Continent with the most rain forest land   a. Okapi
2. World's largest rain forest river   b. Africa
3. Zebra-like rain forest animal   c. Blue Morpho
4. Rain forest butterfly   d. Amazon
5. Continent that's home to the Congo Rain Forest   e. South America

Jungle Journey
This scientist has gotten lost in the rain forest.
Can you help her find the way back to her canoe?

Start

Finish

Twin Toucans
Which two toucan pictures are exactly alike?

A

B

C

D

What's in a Name?

Does Al Abama live in Mobile?

Does Clem N. Tine have appeal?

And what about Mr. Joe King—

Do you think he's serious about

    anything?

All these people I wonder about,

Like Hammond Cheese and Carrie Out.

And Hedda Hair and Douglas Fur.

And Tom Ato—I could go on—

But for now, I'll just let names blur

And give my alphabet soup another stir.

by Ann Nonomus

Name Game

Can you match the correct author's name to each book?

Always Be Prepared	by Earl Lee
How to Write a Best Seller	by Rose Bush
Snakes of the Jungle	by Ada Lot
Tumbling Made Easy	by Anna Conda
How to Make a Movie	by Justin Case
Never Be Late Again	by Jim Nast
How I Solve Baffling Mysteries	by Bea Strong
You Can Be a Weight Lifter	by Holly Wood
Wild Felines of North America	by Paige Turner
Stop and Smell the Flowers	by Duncan Score
A Math Story	by I. Guess
My Life as a Basketball Star	by Bob Katz

Test Your Knight Know-How

Go on a quest for knowledge. Circle your answers and see how many of these questions you can get knight, er, right!

1. What is it called when knights fight on horseback?
   a. Jousting
   b. Rousting
   c. Horsing around

2. What title does a knight often receive?
   a. Your Honor
   b. Sir
   c. Helmet Head

3. What type of a table did King Arthur and his knights use?
   a. Rectangular table
   b. Round table
   c. Times table

4. What is a knight's "code of contact" known as?
   a. Chivalry
   b. Silvery
   c. Drudgery

5. What did a knight's suit of armor typically weigh?
   a. 5 pounds
   b. 50 pounds
   c. 500 pounds

6. A boy beginning knight training, usually at age 7, was known as:
   a. A sage
   b. A page
   c. A paragraph

Answers: 1. a, 2. b, 3. b, 4. a, 5. b, 6. b.

Good Knights

Once upon a time, four knights went out on quests: one to rescue a princess, one to find the Grail, one to capture a dragon, and one to wrestle an ogre. When they returned, they told their tales to the jester, who was supposed to tell the king. But the jester jumbled the tales. Using the clues below, help him sort out who did what.

Use the chart to keep track of your answers. Put an **X** in each box that can't be true and an **O** in boxes that match.

	Dragon	Grail	Ogre	Princess
Erec				
Lancelot				
Gareth				
Percy				

1. The princess got engaged to her rescuer.

2. The ogre was waiting in a tall tower.

3. Percy and Gareth are both happily married.

4. The knight whose name begins with the twelfth letter of the alphabet brought back the Grail.

5. Gareth ended his quest in a cave.

Illustrated by Dan McGeehan

13

Out of This World Funnies

What did the astronomer do when she won the lottery?
She thanked her lucky stars!

Why did the moon say no to dessert?
Because it was full.

How do astronauts serve dinner?
On flying saucers.

What is soft and white and comes from Mars?
Martian-mallows.

What do planets do for fun?
They sing Neptunes.

What do astronauts use to brush their teeth?
Toothspace.

Knock, knock.
Who's there?
Jupiter.
Jupiter who?
Jupiter fly in my soup?

"Could I sit by the window?"

Star Sums

The stars in the Triangulator Galaxy have aligned in a brilliant way. See if you can help them really shine. Fill in each star with one of the numbers from 1 to 19. The three stars that make up the side of each triangle should total 22. No number will appear more than once. We've put in a few numbers to start you off. Fill in the rest, and you are a stellar solver!

High Five!

Just for fun, we've found some famous fives. See how far you can get figuring out these things that have to do with the number five.

1. A hand has 5 of these:

_____

2. This shape has 5 sides:

_____

3. This is the 5th month in the calendar:

_____

4. A normal school week has 5 of these:

_____

5. Your body has 5 of these, which include hearing and touch:

_____

6. There are 5 of these in the "12 Days of Christmas":

_____

7. The alphabet has 5 of these:

_____

8. The United States has 5 of these large bodies of water:

_____

Try 5

1. Name three animals that might live in trees.

2. Circle the fruit that has one large pit.

3. Name two words that rhyme with "light."

4. The Spanish word "caramelo" means camel.
○ True   ○ False

5. Name three animals that are black and white.

Illustrated by Kelly Kennedy

Will the Real Dog Please Stand Up?

Each pair below contains one dog and one fraud. Can you keep yourself out of the doghouse by circling the real dog in each set?

border collie **OR** hoarder collie ?

greenhound **OR** greyhound ?

Labrador taker **OR** Labrador retriever ?

sheepdog **OR** goatdog ?

Irish setter **OR** Irish stander ?

spotweiler **OR** rottweiler ?

pharaoh hound **OR** Cleopatra hound ?

chow chow **OR** eat eat ?

pointer **OR** shaker ?

snippet **OR** whippet ?

Illustrated by Kelly Kennedy

Illustrated by Jim Steck

Uptown Dog

Fifi just moved into this fantastic 12-room doghouse. How can Fifi get from the front door to the back door by going through each room only once?

Picky, Picky

Toothpicks aren't just for teeth anymore! Use letters in the word TOOTHPICKS to spell new, shorter words. For example, the words TOT, POT, and COT are all in there. See how many other words you can form.

TOOTHPICKS

tot

pot

cot

Tricky Sticks

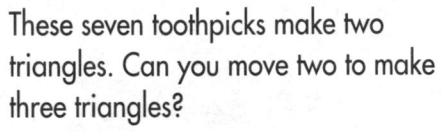

You'll have to "stick to it" if you want to solve these puzzles. For the first two, the toothpicks you need to move are marked in **red**. After that, you'll have to figure it out for yourself!

1 Here are eight toothpicks. Can you make two boxes by moving just two?

Hint: try moving these!

2 These seven toothpicks make two triangles. Can you move two to make three triangles?

3 Move just two toothpicks to turn this shape upside down.

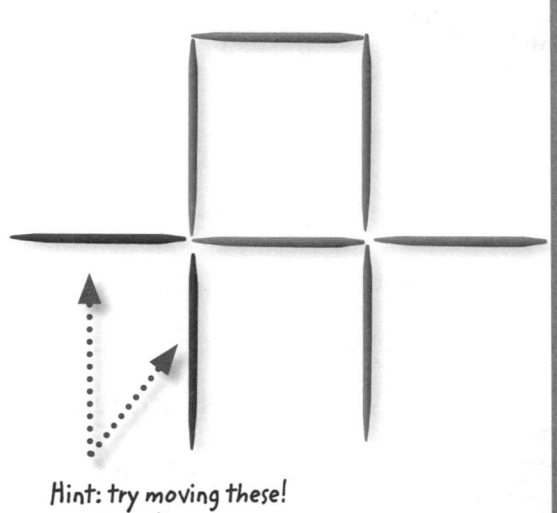

4 Move two toothpicks so this house faces a different direction.

Illustrated by Hey Kids!

Barracuda

Barracuda, barracuda.
Fangs go snapping
in the dark.
Some people fear
the barracuda
more than any shark.
Others say
the fish is cool
unless you have annoyed it.
I say don't take chances.
Barracuda?
Just avoid it.

by Eileen Spinelli

Illustrated by Ron Zalme

Fish Q s

Illustrated by Mike Moran

Start

Finish

So Many Fish in the Sea . . .

Can you unscramble the letters to name the fish?

_____
AUNT

_____
UTROT

_____
KRASH

_____
SFORDWISH

_____
SLMONA

_____
CITSHAF

_____
WINNOM

_____
LOUDFERN

What's in a Name?

The fish with the longest name in the world is called a lauwiliwilinukunukuoioi, in Hawaiian. What do you think it means in English?

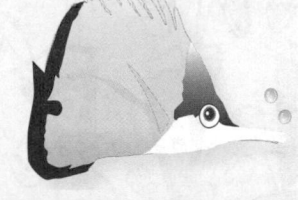

A. Feather-Top Banana Fish
B. Bug-Eye Rock Fish
C. Long-Nosed Butterfly Fish

23

Lucky Laughs

Illustrated by Kelly Kennedy

When is it very bad luck to see a black cat?
When you're a mouse.

Gym teacher: Why aren't you running laps?
Boy: I get enough exercise just pushing my luck!

What do you get when you cross poison ivy with a four-leaf clover?
A rash of good luck.

Knock, knock.
Who's there?
Luck.
Luck who?
Luck through the keyhole and you'll find out!

"You don't know how lucky you are. I have to take him for a walk every night."

Lucky Lists

Feeling lucky? Then this is the puzzle for you! Here are two lists of superstitions—some are considered good luck and others bad. We've done one to get you started. See how many more you can straighten out by unscrambling the words in capital letters. **Good luck!**

GOOD LUCK

SEVEN

The number **VEENS**

Four-leaf **REVOCL**

Face-up **NYPEN**

A turkey **SHIWNOBE**

A **STABRIB** foot

Wishing on a **GNOOSHTI** star

BAD LUCK

Walking under a **REDLAD**

Stepping on a **ELKWIDAS** crack

Breaking a **RIMORR**

Opening an **BREALMUL** indoors

A **CAKBL TAC**

DAFRYI the **NERETHITTH**

Rhyme Time!

Try this quiz on for size. Can you rise to the challenge and figure out the answer to each clue that lies below? Each answer rhymes with PRIZE.

1. Potato snack: French _____

2. Glasses can help these see better: _____

3. Weeps: _____

4. Baked treats with crusts and fillings like pumpkin or cherry: _____

5. Pesky common insects: House _____

6. Boys and men: _____

7. Purchases something at a store: _____

8. Smart: _____

9. Where pigs live: _____

10. Use these to color eggs or hair: _____

Answers: 1. fries, **2.** eyes, **3.** cries, **4.** pies, **5.** flies, **6.** guys, **7.** buys, **8.** wise, **9.** sties, **10.** dyes

Surprise Prize

You've won a prize in the school raffle! But first you have to figure out which item is yours. Follow the directions below to claim your prize!

1. The number on your item is not divisible by 5.

2. The number 3 does not appear on your item's tag.

3. There are three even digits in your item's number.

4. The digits in your prize's number add up to 22.

Illustrated by Wendy Wax

Musical Lingo

Do you know your clef from your coda? Circle each answer and see how your music language stacks up. Ready, set, play!

1. How many musicians are in a duet?
- **a.** Two
- **b.** Four
- **c.** Four hundred

2. Which of the following has the deepest sound range?
- **a.** Alto
- **b.** Baritone
- **c.** Monotone

3. The symbol p means to play an instrument:
- **a.** Quietly
- **b.** Loudly
- **c.** Badly

4. The symbol f means to play an instrument:
- **a.** Quietly
- **b.** Loudly
- **c.** While eating French fries

5. Presto means to play the music:
- **a.** Fast
- **b.** Slow
- **c.** Magically

6. A whole note equals which of these?
- **a.** Three quarter notes
- **b.** Two half notes
- **c.** One sticky note

7. Which is a pair of woodwind instruments?
- **a.** Clarinet and trumpet
- **b.** Flute and oboe
- **c.** Kazoo and bongo drums

Answers: 1. a, 2. b, 3. a, 4. b, 5. a, 6. b, 7. b

Jam Session

Rory and her friends entered their band, Jam Session, in the school talent show. After every practice, the girls have a snack of jam and toast. Using the clues below, can you figure out which instrument each friend plays and what her favorite flavor of jam is?

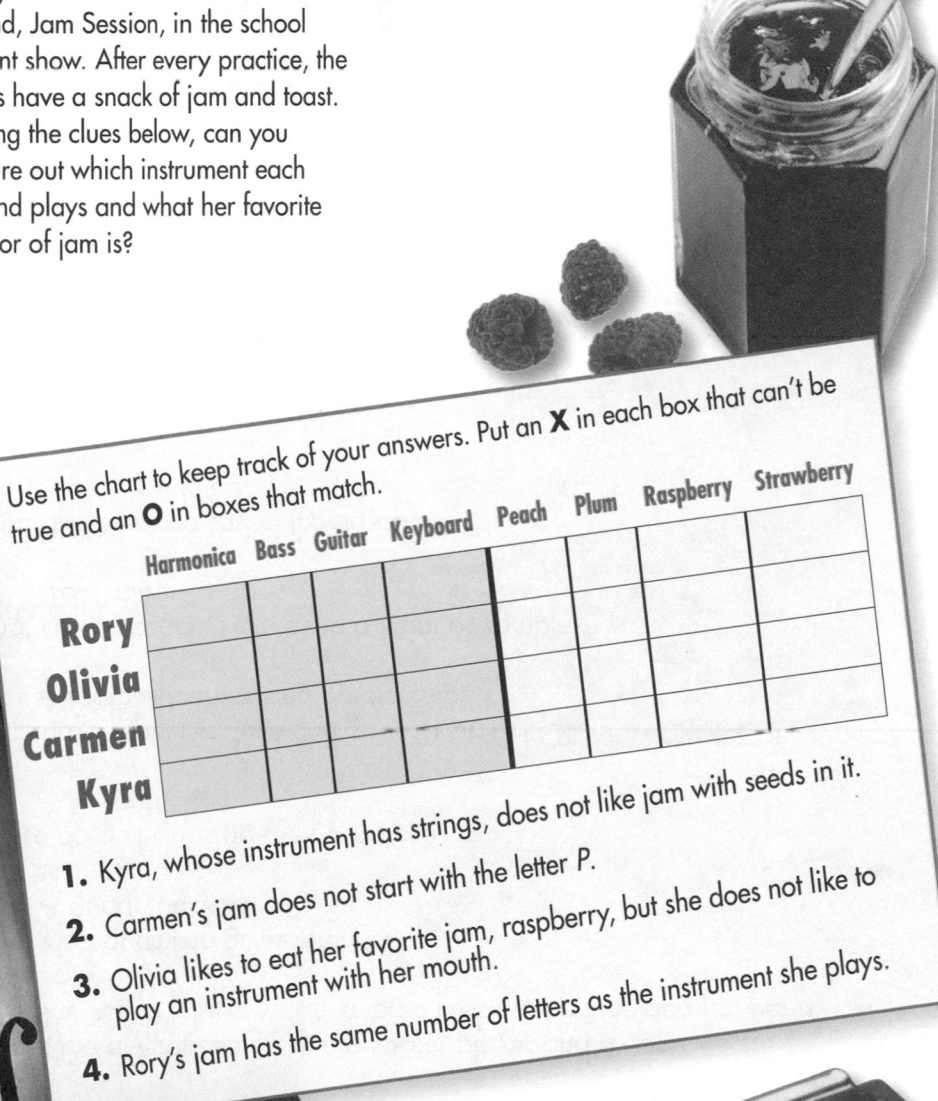

Use the chart to keep track of your answers. Put an **X** in each box that can't be true and an **O** in boxes that match.

	Harmonica	Bass	Guitar	Keyboard	Peach	Plum	Raspberry	Strawberry
Rory								
Olivia								
Carmen								
Kyra								

1. Kyra, whose instrument has strings, does not like jam with seeds in it.

2. Carmen's jam does not start with the letter P.

3. Olivia likes to eat her favorite jam, raspberry, but she does not like to play an instrument with her mouth.

4. Rory's jam has the same number of letters as the instrument she plays.

Puzzle by Sarah Greco

Sports Sillies

What is a pig's favorite position in baseball?
Snortstop.

What's the difference between a soccer player and a dog?
The soccer player wears a team uniform, and the dog just pants.

What kind of athlete gives refunds?
A quarterback.

Where do golf clubs go after a game?
A tee party.

What has twenty-two legs and goes CRUNCH CRUNCH CRUNCH?
A football team eating potato chips.

What can't a coach ever say to a team of zombies?
"Look alive!"

What did the glove say to the baseball?
"Catch you later!"

"I won the 2014 marathon in 2015."

Scramblers

Six sports are hidden in these letters. To find out what they are, first find each group of letters that look the same. Then unscramble each group to find the name of a sport.

Illustrated by Jim Steck

1 _____

2 _____

3 _____

4 _____

5 _____

6 _____

Tongue Tied!

**Try these froggy tongue twisters.
Can you say each five times fast?
Hop to it!**

Frankie's fabulous frog ate frozen fly fondue.

Freckle-faced frogs fidget.

Felicia and Freddy find frogs on Friday.

Five frantic frogs fled from fifty fierce fish.

Four flying frogs flip-flop festively.

Friendly fleas and frogs.

Tic Tac Row

Each of these frogs has something in common with the other two frogs in the same row. For example, in the first row across all three frogs have stripes. Look at the other rows across, down, and diagonally. Can you tell what's alike in each row?

Illustrated by Carolina Farias

Give Me Space!

Test your space know-how with an out-of-this-world quiz. If you can answer all the questions, give yourself a gold star!

1. Pluto is known as this.
   a. A dwarf planet
   b. A baby planet
   c. A puppy planet

2. Which planet is closest to the sun?
   a. Mercury
   b. Venus
   c. Earth

3. How much bigger is the sun's diameter than that of Earth?
   a. 19 times bigger
   b. 109 times bigger
   c. 19 million times bigger

4. What are Saturn's rings made up of?
   a. Ice, dust, and rocks
   b. Fiery gas
   c. Gold and diamonds

5. A quasar is:
   a. Far away and very bright
   b. Far away and very dark
   c. Afraid of the dark

6. What year did astronauts first walk on the moon?
   a. 1949
   b. 1969
   c. 1999

7. What is a common nickname for Mars?
   a. The Red Planet
   b. The Green Planet
   c. E.T.'s Home Planet

Answers: 1. a, 2. a, 3. b, 4. a, 5. a, 6. b, 7. a

Scrambled Space

Need more space? You've come to the right place!
Unscramble these space words. Once you have
them all straightened out, read down the column
of boxes to learn the answer to this riddle:

What do you get when you cross a galaxy and a toad?

Clue	Answer
RAMS	`M` `A` `R` `S`
METCO	☐ _ _ _ _
UNRATS	☐ _ _ _ _ _
RITBO	☐ _ _ _ _
LYMIK YAW	_ _ _ _ ☐ _ _ _
CLABK LOEH	_ _ _ _ ☐ _ _ _
TIPJUER	☐ _ _ _ _ _ _
DREATSIO	_ _ _ ☐ _ _ _ _
SNUVE	_ _ ☐ _ _

Illustrated by Dave Clegg

Arrive at Five

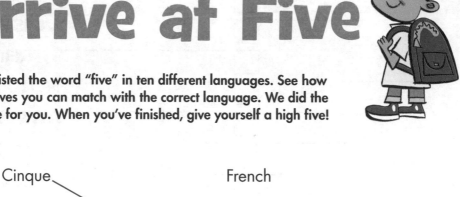

We've listed the word "five" in ten different languages. See how many fives you can match with the correct language. We did the first one for you. When you've finished, give yourself a high five!

Cinque   French

Cinco   German

Fem   Italian

Cinq   Japanese

Go   Mandarin Chinese

Tano   Greek

Beş   Spanish

Wǔ   Swahili

Pende   Swedish

Fünf   Turkish

1. Name two words that rhyme with lake.

2. There are three feet in a yard.
○ True   ○ False

3. Name three planets in our solar system.

4. The Spanish word for school is "escuela."
○ True   ○ False

5. In what country will you most likely see a camel?
○ Iceland   ○ Egypt   ○ Brazil

Illustrated by Kelly Kennedy

Map Laughs

Where can you find an ocean without water?
On a map.

What do map-makers grow in their gardens?
Compass roses.

How does Bigfoot know all the map symbols?
Because he's a legend.

What happened when the cow forgot to pack her map?
She got udder-ly lost!

What do fish and maps have in common?
They both have scales.

What is the tallest road?
The highway.

Teacher: Bailey, please point to America on the map.
Bailey: This is it right here.
Teacher: Well done! Now, class, who discovered America?
Class: Bailey did!

Illustrated by Kelly Kennedy

Map Mix-Up

People are flocking to Logicville for the big Summer Festival. Unfortunately, the new town maps were printed without labels on most of the buildings on Main Street. To help the lost tourists, read the clues below to figure out which building is which. Fill in the correct names on the map.

1. Archie's Arcade is one building south of the Sandwich Hut.

2. Izzy's Ice Cream is northeast of Archie's Arcade.

3. The Movie Palace is north of Sim's Sweets.

4. The T-Shirt Shack is one building south of Izzy's.

Illustrated by Garry Colby   Puzzle by Sara Matson

STOP -Sign List

A stop sign has eight sides. We've rounded up some other famous eights. See how far you can get figuring out these things that have to do with the number eight.

1. This animal has 8 tentacles: _____

2. This is the 8th month in the calendar: _____

3. This shape has 8 sides: _____

4. Arachnids have 8 of these: _____

5. This December holiday lasts for 8 days and 8 nights: _____

6. Santa's sleigh is pulled by 8 of these: _____

7. A skater might be able to form this shape on the ice: _____

8. There are 8 of these in a gallon: _____

Illustrated by Jack Desrocher

Answers: 1. octopus, **2.** August, **3.** octagon, **4.** legs, **5.** Hanukkah, **6.** reindeer, **7.** figure eight, **8.** pints

Stop, Look, and List

Are you ready for a trivia challenge? Fill in each box with a name or word. It must begin with the letter at the top of the column. We put in a few of our favorites to get you started.

CATEGORY	S	T	O	P
Zoo animals				
Kitchen objects				
Words with TT in them			otter	
Art words	sculpture			
Pets' names				Princess
School words			organizer	
Silly salad ingredients		toasted tennis shoes		
Shapes				

Fish Funnies

What kind of music should a person listen to while fishing?
Something catchy!

What do sharks eat at cookouts?
Clamburgers.

Who did the fish give a Valentine to?
His gill-friend.

Why did the shark spit out the clown?
Because he tasted funny.

Why do fish swim in schools?
Because they can't walk.

What do you get if you cross a fish with an elephant?
Swimming trunks.

What is stranger than seeing a catfish?
Seeing a fish bowl.

Go Fish!

Newt works after school at the pet shop. His job is refilling the fishbowls on the shelves. Each type of fish has its own bowl. When Newt is finished, every row up and down, across, and diagonally will have **15** total fish. Can you figure out where each fish goes?

43

Soccer to 'em

Whether you are a soccer fanatic or a newbie to the sport, try this quiz on for size. Can you kick out all the correct answers?

1. What are you required to wear to play organized soccer?
  a. Shorts
  b. Shinguards
  c. A smile

2. Who is the official that makes the calls in soccer?
  a. Umpire
  b. Referee
  c. Your principal

3. What position, on average, runs the most?
  a. Midfielder
  b. Forward
  c. Goalie

4. What is soccer's world championship game called?
  a. World Cup
  b. International Cup
  c. Super Bowl

5. How is a soccer game started?
  a. Throw-in
  b. Kickoff
  c. First pitch

6. The goalie is the only player who can touch the ball with what?
  a. Hands
  b. Head
  c. Armpit

7. Soccer balls come in different sizes. What size ball do professionals use?
  a. 3
  b. 5
  c. XL

Answers: 1. b, 2. b, 3. a, 4. a, 5. b, 6. a, 7. b

Tic Tac Row

Each of these soccer players has something in common with the other two soccer players in the same row. For example, in the first row across all three players have a soccer ball. Look at the other rows across, down, and diagonally. Can you tell what's alike in each row?

45

Get Your Fruits and Veggies!

Eight kinds of fruits and vegetables are hiding in the sentences below. Can you find each one? We did the first one to get you started. Dig right in!

1. Don't forget to clap pleasantly.

2. I saw a pale monster over there.

3. Abe and Lea are team captains.

4. The décor needs to be changed.

5. Ali means well, but sometimes she forgets.

6. Otto ran gently down the hill.

7. The extra snack in the car rotted.

8. Never spin a checker too fast.

Illustrated by Mike Moran

Let's Do Lunch

Leo and his friends each picked a different lunch today. From the clues below, can you figure out which main course and which dessert each friend ordered?

Use the chart to keep track of your answers. Put an **X** in each box that can't be true and an **O** in boxes that match.

	Chicken Sandwich	Hamburger	Mac & Cheese	Spaghetti & Meatballs	Vegetarian Chili	Apple	Ice cream	Orange	Pear	Pudding
Leo										
Ursula										
Nick										
Chloe										
Henry										

1. The two girls each had a sandwich.

2. Leo and Henry both had vegetarian lunches and fruit for dessert.

3. Nick's and Leo's desserts start with the same letter.

4. The friend who had the apple also had the mac & cheese.

5. Ursula doesn't eat red meat, and she always gets an orange.

Amusing Math

Why did the girl always wear her glasses during math class?
> *Because they improve di-vision!*

What did the zero say to the eight?
> *"Nice belt!"*

Why did the math book see the doctor?
> *It had problems.*

Why don't math teachers like to take their shoes off?
> *Because they have square feet.*

Logic Laughs

A woman has seven daughters and each daughter has a brother. How many children does the woman have all together?
> *Eight.*

Lily said, "I was seven years old on my last birthday, and I'll be nine years old on my next birthday." How can this be true?
> *Lily turned eight today.*

Two fathers and two sons order three sandwiches. Each person gets a sandwich. How?
> *There are only three people: a grandfather, a father, and a son.*

How can you go without sleep for seven days?
> *Sleep at night!*

Totally!

Ms. Digit's daughter loves to play with numbers. For fun today, she put together these lists. See if you can figure out which list gives you the largest answer. When you've got that, write the shaded letters from that list in order from right to left and top to bottom in the spaces below to find out Ms. Digit's daughter's first name.

1

- Number of Snow White's dw**A**rfs.
- **M**inus the number of littl**E** pigs.
- Multip**L**ied by the number of innings **I**n a regular major league baseball game.
- Divided by **A** dozen.

TOTAL: _____

2

- Number of days in Au**G**ust.
- Minus the po**I**nts of a half-court basket in basketball.
- Divide**D** by the number of quarts in a **G**allon
- Plus th**E** number of sides on an oc**T**agon.

TOTAL: _____

3

- Age w**H**en you become **A** teenager.
- Plus the **N**umber of letters in the alphabet.
- Divided by the **N**umber of singers in **A** trio.
- Minus the number of sides on a **H**exagon.

TOTAL: _____

Ms. Digit's daughter's first name is: __ __ __ __ __ __

Illustrated by Mike Moran

Hide and Seek!

What's hiding in our puzzle's title? That's for you to find out! Use letters in the words HIDDEN PAIRS to spell new, shorter words. For example, the words DIP, SAP, and SIDE are all in there. See how many other words you can form.

HIDDEN PAIRS

dip

sap

side

Illustrated by Dan McGeehan

Hidden Pairs

Each pair of words below is hiding something. Look closely and you'll find a pair of shorter but related words in the original pair. For example, in the first pair you can find **on** and **off**. Can you spot the other hidden pairs?

1. **s**ong, **c**offee
2. **g**rouping, **l**andowner
3. **h**aunted, **u**nclear
4. **t**highbone, **m**ayflower
5. **h**oliday, **k**nighthood
6. **s**hortcut, **t**otally
7. **p**hotograph, **s**colded
8. **h**ammerhead, **s**nail
9. **m**erchandise, **b**arefooted
10. **f**ishbowl, **s**parrow
11. **a**rchitect, **a**dmission
12. **r**efunded, **b**allgames

Reptile Rib-Ticklers

What did the snake give to his child?
A goodnight hiss.

What do you call an alligator who is wearing a vest?
An investigator.

Snake #1: Are we venomous?
Snake #2: Yes. Why?
Snake #1: I just bit my lip!

How does a rooster wake up a crocodile?
He says, "Croc-a-doodle-doo!"

What reptile stays awake at night and sleeps during the day?
A nocturtle.

Why is it hard to trick a snake?
You can't pull its leg!

Knock, knock.
Who's there?
Iguana.
Iguana who?
Iguana hold your hand.

Reptile Qs

Later, 'Gator

This alligator wants to soak up some sun. Can you help him reach his favorite spot?

Start

Finish

Reptile Report

Some of these reptile facts are true and some are false. Can you tell which are true?

a. All reptiles are cold-blooded.

T or F

b. All reptiles lay eggs.

T or F

c. The Komodo dragon is the smallest species of lizard.

T or F

d. Snakes are able to smell with their tongues.

T or F

Reptile or Amphibian?

Some of these are reptiles and some are amphibians. Can you circle the reptiles?

LIZARD or SALAMANDER ?

NEWT or IGUANA ?

TREE FROG or SEA TURTLE ?

SKINK or TOAD ?

PYTHON or MUDPUPPY ?

53

Puzzles by Carly Schuna   Illustrated by Mike Moran

G Whiz!

Take a gander at these g-word tongue twisters.
Can you say each five times fast without garbling them?
Go on, give it a go!

Girl gargoyle, guy gargoyle.

Grow Greek grapes.

Great Grandma Gertie's
geese giggle.

The glum groom grew glummer.

Gale's great glass globe
glows green.

Great gray goats.

Gus goes by Blue Goose bus.

Gobs of Gibbles

These Gibbles all have some things in common.

None of these are Gibbles.

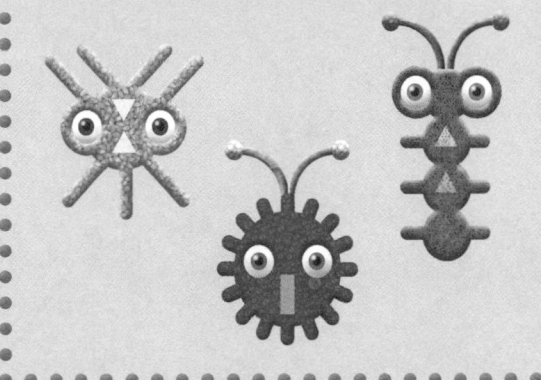

Can you figure out which of these are Gibbles?

Illustrated by Paul Richer

Money Match-Up

Here's a different kind of treasure hunt. Can you match each of these types of money with the country where it is used?

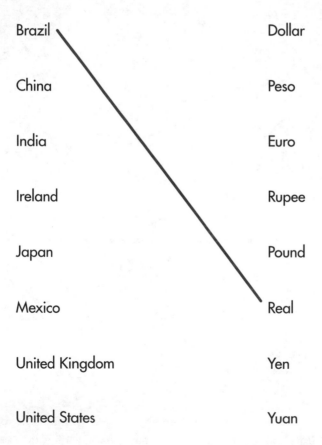

Brazil	Dollar
China	Peso
India	Euro
Ireland	Rupee
Japan	Pound
Mexico	Real
United Kingdom	Yen
United States	Yuan

Treasure Hunt

Can you find a path to the buried treasure? Start at the **5** in the top corner. You may move to a new box by **adding 5** or by **subtracting 3**. Move up, down, left, or right.

Start

5	10	17	10	7	12
5	7	12	13	4	9
11	6	9	8	21	18
16	19	6	11	16	15
13	18	20	12	21	12
10	15	17	15	20	17

Finish

Illustrated by Dave Klug

Robot Laughs

Why was the robot angry?
Because someone kept pushing his buttons.

What is a robot's favorite music?
Heavy metal.

When is a robot like a surgeon?
When it operates on batteries.

How did the scientist fix the robot gorilla?
With a monkey wrench.

What do you call a robot that always takes the longest route?
R2-Detour.

What is a robot's favorite type of food?
Vegetabolts.

Who did the robot share her secrets with?
Her most rusted friend.

Tic Tac Row

Each of these robots has something in common with the other two robots in the same row. For example, in the first row across all three robots are on wheels. Look at the other rows across, down, and diagonally. Can you tell what's alike in each row?

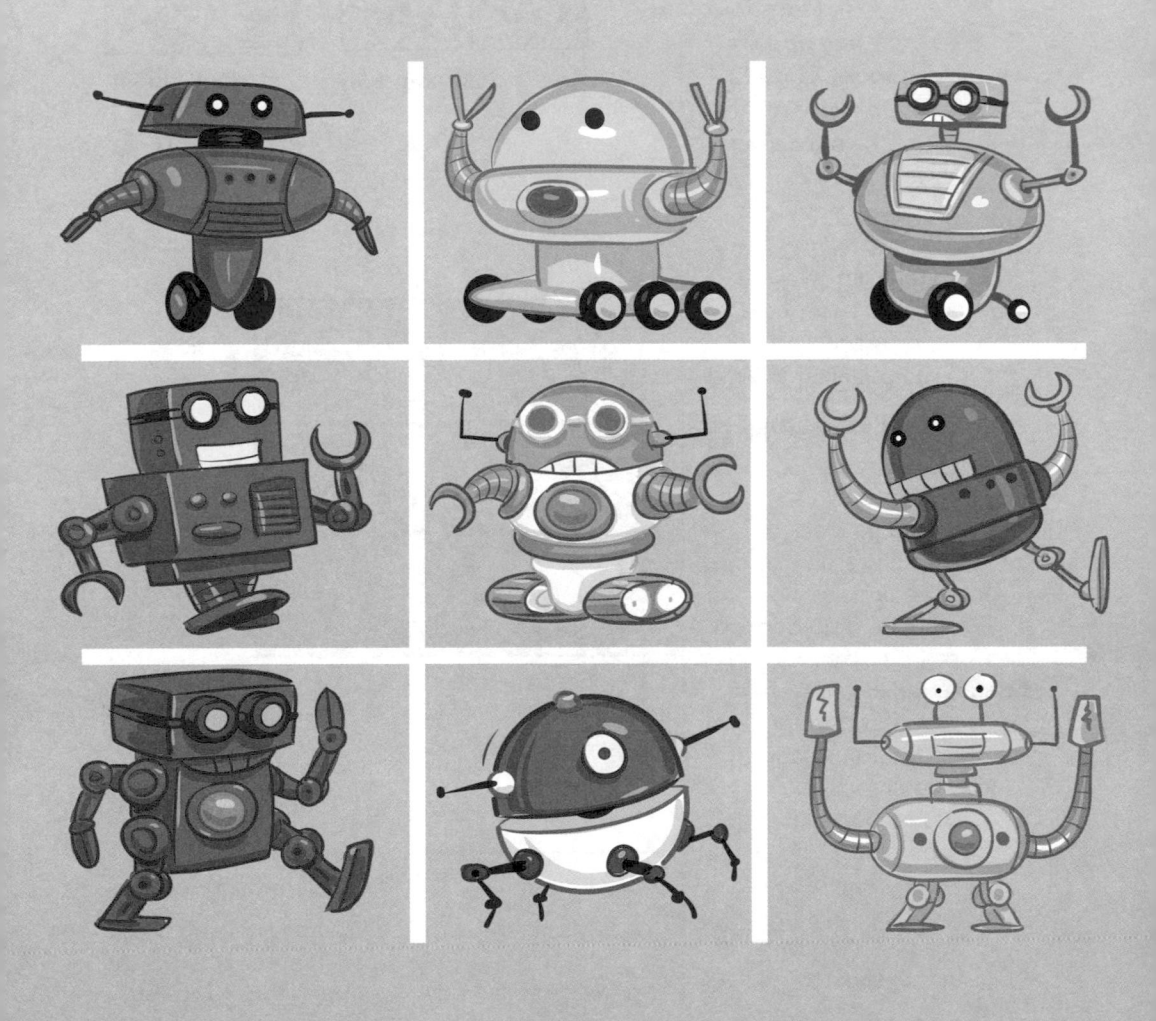

Illustrated by Dave Clegg

Answers

1 If at First . . .

What do you get when you cross a monster and a baseball game?

A DOUBLEHEADER

3 Doggie Dilemma

Diego picks a BEAGLE.

5 Tic Tac Row

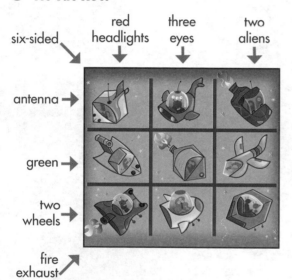

six-sided, red headlights, three eyes, two aliens

antenna

green

two wheels

fire exhaust

9 Rain Forest Q's

Jungle Journey

Twin Toucans

Rain Forest Quiz

1. e
2. d
3. a
4. c
5. b

7 Say What?

1. 60 seconds in a minute
2. 7 days in a week
3. 12 inches in a foot
4. 12 months in a year
5. 4 quarts in a gallon
6. 2 cups in a pint
7. 60 minutes in an hour
8. 3 feet in a yard
9. 24 hours in a day
10. 26 letters in the alphabet
11. 52 weeks in a year
12. 365 days in a year
13. 100 years in a century
14. 52 cards in a deck
15. 50 stars on the U.S. flag

11 Name Game

Always Be Prepared
   by Justin Case
How to Write a Best Seller
   by Paige Turner
Snakes of the Jungle
   by Anna Conda
Tumbling Made Easy
   by Jim Nast
How to Make a Movie
   by Holly Wood
Never Be Late Again
   by Earl Lee
How I Solve Baffling Mysteries
   by I. Guess
You Can Be a Weight Lifter
   by Bea Strong
Wild Felines of North America
   by Bob Katz
Stop and Smell the Flowers
   by Rose Bush
A Math Story
   by Ada Lot
My Life as a Basketball Star
   by Duncan Score

Answers

13 Good Knights

Erec: Princess
Lancelot: Grail
Gareth: Dragon
Percy: Ogre

15 Star Sums

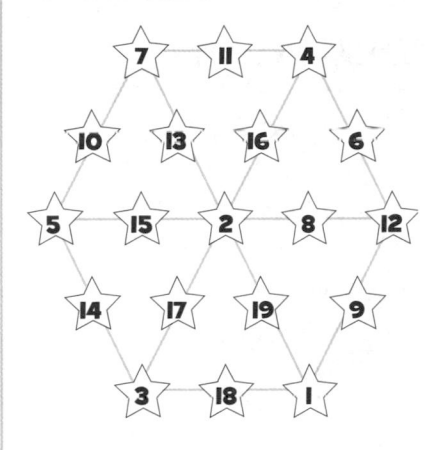

7 11 4
10 13 16 6
5 15 2 8 12
14 17 19 9
3 18 1

17 Try 5

1. Owl, squirrel, and monkey. Did you think of others?
2. Circle the peach. It has one large pit.
3. Knight and kite
4. False. "Caramelo" means candy.
5. Penguin, skunk, and panda

19 Uptown Dog

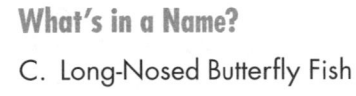

21 Tricky Sticks

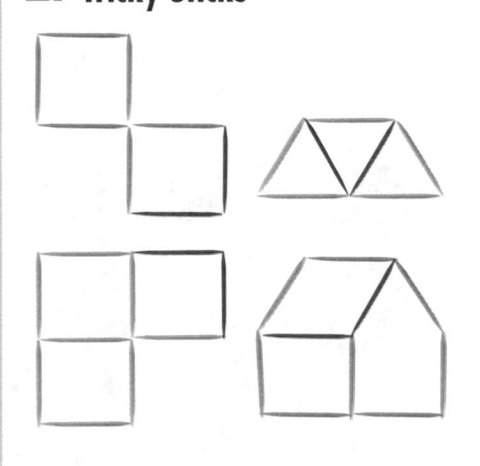

23 Fish Q's

What's in a Name?

C. Long-Nosed Butterfly Fish

So Many Fish in the Sea...

TUNA
TROUT
SHARK
SWORDFISH
SALMON
CATFISH
MINNOW
FLOUNDER

School of Fish

Answers

25 Lucky List

Good Luck
The number SEVEN
Four-leaf CLOVER
Face-up PENNY
A turkey WISHBONE
A RABBIT'S foot
Wishing on a SHOOTING star

Bad Luck
Walking under a LADDER
Stepping on a SIDEWALK crack
Breaking a MIRROR
Opening an UMBRELLA inside
A BLACK CAT
FRIDAY the THIRTEENTH

31 Scramblers

1. BASEBALL
2. HOCKEY
3. FOOTBALL
4. TENNIS
5. LACROSSE
6. SOCCER

35 Scrambled Space

MARS
COMET
SATURN
ORBIT
MILKY WAY
BLACK HOLE
JUPITER
ASTEROID
VENUS

What do you get when you cross a galaxy and a toad?
STAR WARTS

27 Surprise Prize

The skateboard is the prize.

29 Jam Session

Rory: bass, plum jam
Olivia: keyboard, raspberry jam
Carmen: harmonica, strawberry jam
Kyra: guitar, peach jam

33 Tic Tac Row

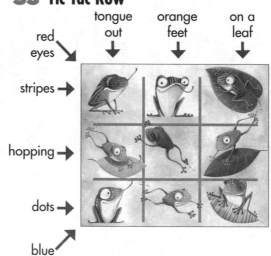

37 Try 5

1. Snake and cake rhyme with lake. Did you think of others?
2. True
3. Earth, Mars, and Saturn
4. True
5. Egypt

39 Map Mix-Up

Movie Palace—Sandwich Hut—Izzy's Ice Cream
Sim's Sweets—Archie's Arcade—T-Shirt Shack

Answers

41 Stop, Look, and List

Here are some possible answers. You may have thought of others.

Zoo animals—snake, tiger, orangutan, panda
Kitchen objects—spoon, toaster, oven, pan
Words with "TT" in them—settle, tattle, otter, pretty
Art words—sculpture, tracing paper, oil paints, portrait
Pets' names—Sparky, Torpedo, Oscar, Princess
School words—study, test, organizer, pencil
Silly salad ingredients—scrambled sardines, toasted tennis shoes, oatmeal, pan-fried peppermint
Shapes—square, triangle, octagon, pentagon

43 Go Fish

45 Tic Tac Row

47 Let's Do Lunch

Leo: vegetarian chili, pear
Ursula: chicken sandwich, orange
Nicholas: spaghetti and meatballs, pudding
Chloe: hamburger, ice cream
Henry: mac & cheese, apple

49 Totally!

1. $7 - 3 = 4$
   $4 \times 9 = 36$
   $36 \div 12 = 3$

2. **$31 - 3 = 28$**
   $28 \div 4 = 7$
   $7 + 8 = 15$

3. $13 + 26 = 39$
   $39 \div 3 = 13$
   $13 - 6 = 7$

Ms. Digit's daughter's first name is GIDGET.

51 Hidden Pairs

1. on, off
2. up, down
3. aunt, uncle
4. high, low
5. day, night
6. short, tall
7. hot, cold
8. hammer, nail
9. hand, foot
10. bow, arrow
11. hit, miss
12. fun, games

Answers

53 Reptile Q's

Later, 'Gator

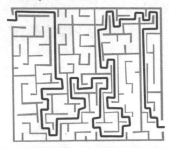

Reptile Report

a. All reptiles are cold-blooded. **T**
b. All reptiles lay eggs. **F**
c. The Komodo dragon is the smallest species of lizard. **F**
d. Snakes are able to smell with their tongues. **T**

Reptile or Amphibian?

LIZARD
IGUANA
SEA TURTLE
SKINK
PYTHON

55 Gobs of Gibbles

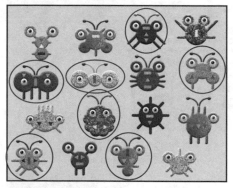

Gibbles have two antennae, two triangles, and one rectangle on their bodies.

57 Treasure Hunt

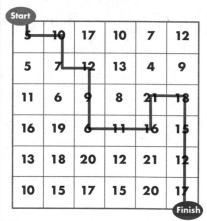

59 Tic Tac Row

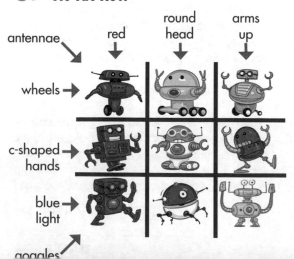